Should Schools Serve Only Healthful Lunches?

by Mrs. Wilson's class
with Tony Stead

capstone classroom

What kinds of lunches do you like? Do you like only healthful foods, or do you like treats? Maybe you like both!

The four students who wrote letters in this book to Dr. Jones, their principal, provide arguments for different kinds of lunches. After you read the letters, think about what kind of food your cafeteria serves. Should the menu be changed? Do any of the students' arguments convince you that schools should serve only healthful lunches? Why or why not?

September 14

Dear Dr. Jones,

I think that our school should serve only healthful lunches. Let me tell you why I feel this way.

One important reason is students usually throw their healthful lunches in the garbage and only eat bad foods. When they don't eat a significant amount of healthful food, they get sick.

Maybe kids could have healthful lunches and dessert. That might resolve the conflict because both foods are healthful.

Mom
girl
I'm sick!
Eat healthey!
Baby

My last reason for our school serving only healthful lunches is that students could get headaches when they get home. This is probably because they didn't eat nutritious foods.

These are my reasons why I think only healthful lunches should be served. Hopefully I convinced you to make some changes.

Sincerely,

Sahana

Headache!

September 14

Dear Dr. Jones,

I think our school should serve only healthful lunches. I hope my arguments will cause a change.

One important reason is that when kids eat unhealthful foods, they don't feel well and they get sick more often. Sometimes I see kids not eating vegetables and eating cookies or other unhealthful food.

Another important reason is that the medical bill is way higher than a healthful lunch cost. So kids are sometimes eating unhealthful food and their families are paying lots of money for the medical bills.

My last significant reason for our school serving only healthful lunches is that some kids don't like the veggies and throw them in the trash because of the taste. But a good way to fix this is to hide vegetables in popular foods or desserts, like brownies with spinach and mac and cheese with broccoli.

These are the reasons why I think only healthful lunches should be served by our school.

Thank you for your consideration.

Sincerely,

Nisha

September 14

Dear Dr. Jones,

I think we should serve only healthful lunches. I have many reasons why.

One important reason is that healthful foods help our bodies. Another important reason is that kids need vitamins and are not getting the nutritious food they need. My last reason for schools serving only nutritious lunches is that these types of lunches help kids stay fit.

In closing, I think that only healthful lunches should be served. Thank you very much for considering these arguments for healthful lunches.

Your student,

Arden

September 14

Dear Dr. Jones,

I think our school should not change its menu to only healthful food. I have many reasons why I feel this way.

One reason is that healthful food costs an enormous amount of money. It might be hazardous to some people to spend a lot, so they may not have an opportunity to eat healthfully. Also, some kids might not like the taste of healthful food, so they wouldn't eat their lunch.

My last reason is that sometimes it's fine to have treats. If we never get treats, we might mope over what we have to eat for lunch.

These are the reasons why I think our lunches shouldn't include only healthful food. Thank you for your consideration in this matter.

Your student,

Gloria

My Lunch Tray
milk

The letters are all different, but the students do want variety in their lunches. Here are some of the foods students would like:

- A generous amount of red fruits and vegetables is wonderful for your heart,
- Blue fruits and vegetables are good for your brain,
- Orange fruits and vegetables are stupendous for your eyes,
- Green fruits and vegetables are good for your health,
- Nuggets because they do not cost a lot, and
- Hot chocolate on very cold days to keep kids happy and warm.

What would you ask for in a letter to your principal about healthful school lunches?